# Introduction to the world of heteromorphs

## Description, history, curiosities and advice on the main breeds found on the market.

A Brief History of Goldfish

What is meant by "Fancy Goldfish"

Fundamental requirements for keeping any goldfish

Fantails

Ryukin

Pompoms

Black Moor and other telescopes

What is "wen"?

Lion head

Ranchu

Oranda

Pearlscale

Bubble eyes

Celestials

Reproduction

Conclusions

# THE AMAZING HISTORY OF THE GOLDFISH: FROM FOOD TO SYMBOL OF IMPERIAL NOBILITY... TO THEN END UP IN AQUARIUMS (AND BOWLS...) ALL OVER THE WORLD.

The exact date in which man, specifically, at least for the purposes of our history, the farmers of the rice fields of ancient China began to raise freshwater fish is not known precisely.

What is certain is that the person who first gave life (as we will see, unconsciously) to the noble art of aquarium keeping did not do so with the aim of filling aquariums or fountains, but rather his own stomach...

The first certain evidence on the

farming of crucian carp and common carp dates back to around 4000 BC. in ancient China, where farmers already raised fish in the rice fields, in perfect synergy with the cultivation of the rice itself, with a symbiotic relationship between the rice plant and fish where the former kept the oxygen levels in the water high, while the latter fertilized literally the crops with their feces.

Fish, mainly cyprinids such as carp and crucian carp, were raised for food, rather than for more ornamental purposes; an abundant and always available, precious source of proteins.

Among these fish we also find one of the possible ancestors of the modern goldfish (Carassius Auratus), namely the Prussian crucian carp (Carassius Gibelio), characterized by silver-colored scales and a generally greyish color.

Prussian crucian carp (By George Chernilevsky - Own work, CC BY-SA 4.0, https://commons.wikimedia.org/w/index.php?curid=105432256), comparison with domestic goldfish (next page).

Another possible wild ancestor of the common goldfish is the common crucian carp (Carassius Carassius) characterized by a more rounded snout than that of the Prussian crucian carp and way more than that of the common goldfish, which is markedly pointed.

Carassius Carassius (By Viridiflavus - Own work, CC BY-SA 3.0, https://commons.wikimedia.org/w/index.php?curid=5694245)

However, according to modern genetic analyses, the modern goldfish appears to be a species in its own right, not particularly related to either of the two wild crucians seen so far, but itself a third species, Carassius Auratus in fact.

Given the high invasiveness of goldfish and crucians in general, the most plausible scenario is that in which the domestic form, orange in color, bred in large quantities over the centuries, has completely replaced the wild form, due to numerous cross paths with the latter.

By the way, the hypothesis cannot be ruled out that the modern crucian carp is actually a hybrid, which also involves other species, such as the Prussian and the common crucian carp, also given the high ease with which the crucian carp cross with each other, generating fertile offspring.

Returning to our history, it was only during the Jin dynasty (266-420 AD) that the appearance of the mutation that makes goldfish orange is attested.

While it was during the Song dynasty (960–1279 AD) that the practice of breeding goldfish, for purely ornamental purposes, in private fountains and ponds, was now rooted within the imperial family.

Each gold-colored crucian carp could ONLY belong to a member of the imperial family, common plebeians, as well as low-ranking nobles, were FORBIDDEN to possess these fascinating, noble, gold-colored creatures.

◆ ◆ ◆

It was only during the 17th century that things began to change to the point that goldfish began to be sold, mainly by the Portuguese and Dutch, around the world.

In 1603, goldfish were introduced by the Dutch to Japan, a country that gave rise, in the following centuries, to a spectacular selection that produced many of the forms of heteromorphic goldfish, including the oranda, which we still see on the market today.

In 1611 they arrived in Portugal and from there to the rest of Europe, initially especially southern Europe and the Mediterranean, where they became a symbol of wealth and good omen… due to the color of gold they wore on their skin.

Giving his wife a goldfish on their first anniversary, as a good omen for a future of wealth together, soon became a common custom for married men.

Finally, the goldfish also arrived in America in 1850, becoming a common pet, especially in the United States.

## WHAT IS A "FANCY" GOLDFISH?

The appearance of mutations concerning the shape of the body in goldfish and, consequently, the appearance of heteromorphic goldfish (literally: "of different shape") is attested in China, under the Ming dynasty (1368–1644) when, thanks to the growing tendency to breed goldfish at home, it was possible to select characteristics that would have compromised the survival of the fish outdoors or, at least, in a context in which they would have to compete for food with "normal" goldfish (homeomorphic, literally: "same shape").

Among these characteristics we find the development of a double tail, the development of a "fatter", rounded and egg-shaped body, and other structures never seen before such as the "wen", or a series of growths that can cover the upper part of the head, or the entire head (we will return to the wen later, in the dedicated chapter: "what is wen?").

When the Dutch brought goldfish to Japan, effectively importing them from China, among these fish there were already some with the characteristics described above.

It was precisely those fishes with stocky bodies and heads covered in wen to attract the attention of the Japanese the most.

Japanese who gave them the name of "Oranda Shishigashira" (オランダ獅子頭), or: "Dutch Lion Head", given the similarity of the wen to a lion's mane and given that the Japanese defined any imported good as "Dutch", at that time.

A pair of Orandas, in this case a "red cap", due to the red color of the wen, on top of the head.

(Image By Rodsan18 at English Wikipedia, CC BY 2.5, https://commons.wikimedia.org/w/index.php?curid=13358663)

A lion's head, characterized by a well developed wen, similar to a raspberry in form, by the lack of dorsal fin and by straight shape of its back.

(Imagine By Lawrencekhoo - Own work, CC BY-SA 4.0, https://commons.wikimedia.org/w/index.php?curid=37240411)

◆ ◆ ◆

In the following four centuries we assist to the creation, due selective breeding, of all the other fancy goldfish breeds: like the Ranchu, the Ryukin, the Black Moor, the bubble eyes and way more.

On the specific breeds, their characteristics, necessities, history and more we'll return later, in this book.

# Fundamental prerequisites before purchasing any goldfish.

-Tank's size and filtering.

-Temperature

-Diet

-Compatibility

◆ ◆ ◆

First of all SPACE, the small goldfish that you buy in the shop are, in all reality, youngsters and as such they grow… and A LOT.

A common goldfish can even exceed 40cm and weigh a few

kilos... an aquarium with a large volume is ideal for these fish.

The rule that you read around, searching on the internet and combing through various dedicated groups on social media, is that in a goldfish aquarium each fish must have at least 60 litres available; therefore, an aquarium with two goldfish (crucians are sociable fish and live better in company, rather than alone) should measure at least 120 litres.

This rule, which in itself is not totally wrong, however only takes into account the needs of a goldfish of the size of those found in the shop, i.e. small fish no longer than 10 cm...

As already mentioned, these little fish are practically puppies, no older than 6-8 months.

It is difficult to make a 30 cm goldfish happy in a tank of only 60 litres... as well as two in a 120.

The ideal habitat for goldfish, to be honest, would in fact be a beautiful pond; a nice outdoor pond, where the animal can grow exploiting its full potential, without therefore becoming stunted... as happens to all goldfish placed in small aquariums or... worse still in bowls, be in full health and even reproduce.

In a pond, a goldfish also develops much more intense colors and brighter scales, thanks to the large quantity of algae, which grow spontaneously due the sun, which it will feed on together with a large number of aquatic insects and more.

But to be brief... ultimately, the pond best expresses all the genetic potential of a goldfish for the simple fact that this is ITS NATURAL HABITAT, in which its wild ancestors lived for millions of years.

◆ ◆ ◆

Returning to our beloved fancy goldfish, or heteromorphic goldfish, they generally require less space than the classic goldfish, BUT NOT TOO MUCH, generally around two thirds of the volume but only because, given the shape of their body, more stocky and clumsy, they tend to swim less, covering less distance, as well as being shorter.

However, we are still talking about goldfish, which, as such, they grow a lot, even beyond 25 cm.

Furthermore... what heteromorphs lack in length, compared to homeomorphs, they make up for in width...

Filtering is another issue of fundamental importance that must be addressed when you want to host crucian carp in your aquarium.

Crucian carp, all crucian carp, are VERY DIRTY, they eat a lot and produce an impressive quantity of faeces which, by decomposing, will pollute the water with a large quantity of nitrates and nitrites which, if not promptly treated and degraded by the filter and its beneficial bacteria, they will reach such a concentration as to poison our fish.

Therefore, the filtering system must be very important, imposing to say the least; a filter with an hourly capacity equal to 3, even 4 times the volume of our tank, represents the standard.

The normal "backpack" filters, those that are hooked inside the aquarium and attached with suction cups, so to speak, do not have the right amount of space to accommodate the large quantity of ceramic razor clams (those white and porous tubes, essential in the filter of every aquarium) and of filter wool necessary to obtain the right amount of bacteria (beneficial bacteria of course), this is essential to cope with the aforementioned large quantities of nitrogenous substances to be eliminated.

The ideal is to equip yourself with an external filter, the kind that is placed in cabinets, to connect to our aquarium.

As regards the "pond" issue, as already mentioned, orandas, although modified by millennia of human selection, are still crucians and, as such, benefit greatly from living outdoors.

However, some precautions must be taken with these fish, which the common goldfish does not require.

First of all, the temperature... at least for the most selected and elaborate forms, which are not capable of withstanding temperatures as low as those tolerated by normal goldfish.

Generally, more specifically, the more different the breed of heteromorph is compared to the starting common goldfish, the more susceptible it will be to low temperatures.

The main cause lies in the fact that, as already explained in the part relating to the history of goldfish, the selection of fancy goldfish has taken place, for centuries, indoors and inside the home.

Therefore, there has been an accumulation of mutations that have led to the loss of the ability, in these animals, to resist the coldest temperatures, as these fish no longer need the "right genes" to survive the frost.

However, it is not a universal rule and there are several "fanatics" of free-range farming who would attack me just for mentioning the topic…

Fanatics who, when it is pointed out

to them that not all fancy goldfish left outdoors manage to survive the winter... respond with excuses regarding "the survival of the fittest" forgetting that we are faced with varieties of fish that are A PRODUCT OF MAN , and which DO NOT EXIST in nature.

The truth is that, if it is true that there are still specimens capable of surviving outdoors, thanks to having inherited the right combination of genes, it is also true that leaving an oranda, a lion head, a black moor or any other fancy goldfish outdoors in winter, without a heater, is equivalent to point a gun at the poor goldfish and "play" Russian roulette with it.

As a fancy goldfish owner and a person who cares about animals, I advise ANYONE against leaving these fish at temperatures below 15 degrees.

You can raise them outdoors, as I was saying your animals would benefit greatly from it, the important thing is to have a heater that keeps the temperature around 15 degrees during the colder months.

Having said this, it is also good to remember that we are still dealing with cold water fish, which, as such, do not require heating when temperatures are higher and, on the contrary! Temperatures that are too high, such as above 26 degrees and especially if all year round, stress our animals quite a bit, causing premature aging and not stimulating the correct sexual maturation, as well as the fregola itself, which is stimulated precisely by the gradual increase of the temperature in spring.

◆ ◆ ◆

Nutrition is another important factor, a real pillar, for the well-being of our fish.

If it is true that goldfish, whatever their variety and shape, are omnivorous animals, capable of eating anything and... I underline ANYTHING (I saw an oranda in a shop trying to eat a piece of trunk...), It is also true that their diet must be complete, varied and COMPATIBLE with their digestive capacities.

First of all, there must be a certain quantity of fiber, which facilitates intestinal transit, especially in heteromorphs with more compact silhouettes, such as oranda, ranchu, lion's head etc... where, due to the stocky shape of the body, the organs are more compressed, the intestinal loops more folded on themselves and therefore prone to becoming clogged, and finally the swim bladder, more susceptible in these forms to various forms of dysfunction, caused by its compression by the intestine, when it is constipated.

Specifically, the swim bladder may have problems deflating, resulting in excessive buoyancy of the fish, which will also tend to tip over in the worst situations, or, on the contrary, it may have problems filling with gas; in the latter case causing excessive sinking of the fish, which will have to work harder than necessary to swim to the surface.

◆ ◆ ◆

Foods rich in fiber are obviously plant-based ones; peas, courgettes, spinach, pumpkin are ideal, once blanched, to give our friends the right dose of fiber, who are, among other things, particularly fond of vegetables and will eagerly eat the aforementioned foods.

Naturally, proteins should never be missing from the diet of our crucian carp.

It is very important to offer them easily digestible proteins, such as those contained in the insects and crustaceans they would feed on in nature.

Blood Worms, or bloodworm larvae, easily available frozen in many shops, are an excellent protein supplement, to be added to the feed together with vegetables.

So let's get to the feed issue... the real sore point of this topic.

There are many industrial feeds on the market, for all budgets and all needs; it is ESSENTIAL to choose the best ones, even at the cost of spending more.

To anyone who objects, I want to remind them that aquarium keeping is a HOBBY and not something "mandatory"... a LUXURY and not something we need like bread...

If you don't have money for an aquarium, to keep it decently and to feed your fish decently... forget it... it's not for you!

The main problem with cheaper (and poorer) feed is the large quantity of CEREALS they use as "fillers"... that is, to bulk up, saving on more expensive ingredients such as fish, crustaceans and insect flour.

Grains are a TERRIBLE food for fish; they are rich in starch and other sugars, macromolecules which almost do not exist in their diet in nature and which, as such, create quite a few problems for their digestive system, first of all the fermentation of the poorly digested sugars themselves (their digestive system It did NOT evolve to digest starch and related sugars efficiently), which leads to bloating, constipation, and the swim bladder problems we discussed earlier.

Any feed with the words "cereals and derivatives" as the first ingredient should immediately be rejected in our choice.

◆ ◆ ◆

Last but not least, compatibility.

There are numerous morphological differences between common and heteromorphic goldfish, as well as between the same varieties of heteromorphs.

These differences affect the animal's ability to swim, see, search and eat food.

It goes without saying that more stocky, elaborate forms and, in a nutshell, more "handicapped" by human selection... will have quite a few problems coexisting in the tank with the more agile, faster and more skilled ones, running the risk of not being able to eat enough because outclassed in the competition by the latter.

Homomorphic goldfish, i.e. classic ones, should not be placed with heteromorphic ones.

But even among heteromorphs there is an abyss in physical differences and in the consequent swimming and/or visual abilities.

We move from the Fantails which,

except for the more rounded body and the double tail, have no other differences with the classic goldfish, up to the bubble eyes which, with their large under-ocular sacs, full of liquid, have great difficulty both in swimming and in seeing and even in eating food…

We will talk in detail about the specific differences and compatibility for each of the varieties examined in this text.

# FANTAIL

A young Fantail.

(Image By Souravgg8 - Own work, CC BY-SA 4.0, https://commons.wikimedia.org/w/index.php?curid=84889262)

- Name: Fantail, Man-yu (in Chinese).
- Origins: Western China, around 1400.
- Breeding difficulty: Low, almost comparable to that of the common goldfish.

The Fantail, literally "fan tail", is the most "basic" form of heteromorphic goldfish, as well as the most common and easily available in pet shops.

The Fantail, except for the presence of a "double" tail (i.e. a tail that ends with two caudal fins) and for the "egg" shape of the body, which is stockier and "fatter", more rounded than the common goldfish, is characterized by an aspect that does not present major differences with the latter.

A "veiltail" Fantail, characterized by long and flowing caudal fins.

(Image By Bkrhodesva - Own work, CC BY-SA 4.0, https://commons.wikimedia.org/w/index.php?curid=37437892

Also common is the subvariety, with long and drooping fins, or "veil fins".

There is a wide range of possible colours, ranging from red to calico, ranging from canary yellow, bronze and black.

As regards the breeding of this variety and its specifications, there are no major differences with the common goldfish, not even regarding the temperature factor during the winter.

Not being a highly selected and "botched" variety of goldfish, it still has numerous traits in common with wild ones, including great adaptability to outdoor life, even in winter and without a heater.

The only precaution I would like to suggest is not to put it in the same aquarium/pond with the common homomorphic goldfish which, by virtue of the more slender body shape and the consequent greater speed and agility in swimming, would have an excessive advantage competitive on poor Fantails during foraging, with the serious risk of malnutrition.

At the same time, since heteromorphic Fantails are not excessively stocky and compact, and do not have any other type of handicap, they should not be placed with heteromorphs of much stockier varieties, "handicapped" by the presence of wen or other bulky structures, or by other type of incapacitation (for example of a visual type, as in telescopic, celestial, etc.) compared to which they would have, this time, an excessive advantage in the search for food.

◆ ◆ ◆

# RYUKIN

A mature specimen of ryukin, note the characteristic well developed hump.

(Image By Lawrencekhoo - Own work, CC BY-SA 4.0, https://commons.wikimedia.org/w/index.php?curid=37240413)

- -Name: Ryukin.
- -Origins: Eastern China and Japan
- -Breeding difficulty: Low

Characterized by a body that develops very high to the point that, in some specimens, the fish can become taller than long (provided the tail is excluded), the Ryukin is distinguished from all other heteromorphs by the shape of the back, which grows forming a characteristic hump, from which the peculiar height development of the animal derives.

Some scholars consider the Fantail and the Ryukin to be the same variety, although they differ greatly in the shape of their backs.

Most, however, believe that they

should be considered two separate breeds, above all due to their different origins, Western China for the Fantail and Eastern China and Japan for the Ryukin.

What gives the ryukin its characteristic, differently shaped back is the lack of some vertebrae in the spine.

The hump grows until it reaches its maximum development as the animal grows; barely perceptible in young specimens, it grows to the point of giving the entire body an almost discoidal shape in more mature specimens.

Another physical characteristic of the Ryukin is the very round and pronounced belly.

There are numerous chromatic varieties for the Ryukin, as well as for the fantail, with liveries ranging from the classic orange, to red and white, up to the calico, passing through the melanistic one.

As regards the shape of the tail, they are divided into two varieties:

- Fantail, where the tail is relatively

short, about as deep as the body

- Ribbontail, where the tail is very long and the four lobes are veiled and flowing to the point of resembling ribbons. It is also poetically called Swallowtail.

◆ ◆ ◆

FANCY GOLDFISH

A Magnificent specimen of Ryukin veiltail of intense red color

(Image By Lerdsuwa - Own photo (400D + 50/1.4), CC BY-SA 3.0, https://commons.wikimedia.org/w/index.php?curid=1781

❖ ❖ ❖

As regards the specific needs of this breed, they do not differ much from those already seen for the Fantails.

The Ryukin are a very robust variety, resistant to the cold and outdoor life, they are also good swimmers, slightly inferior to the common Fantail, with which they have no major problems coexisting.

The ryukin is one of the most important breeds on a historical level in the aquarium world relating to heteromorphic goldfish, as it has been used numerous times for crosses that have led to the birth of other breeds or "sub-varieties" of these; examples are the telescopic ones with an arched back such as the Demekin and varieties of oranda such as the Thai ones obtained from the cross between a Ryukin and a Ranchu.

◆ ◆ ◆

GIUSEPPE BARBONE

# Bent-backed Demekin

Image By Lawrencekhoo - Own work, CC BY-SA 4.0, https://commons.wikimedia.org/w/index.php?curid=37240409

❖ ❖ ❖

Beautiful specimen of Thai Oranda, obtained from crosses involving both the Ranchu and the Ryukin.

(Image By Lawrencekhoo - Own work, CC BY-SA 4.0, https://commons.wikimedia.org/w/index.php?curid=37240422)

◆ ◆ ◆

# POMPOM

(Image By: Lawrencekhoo)

- Names: Pompom, Hana Fusa, 天鹅绒球 (Tiān'éróng qiú) "velvet ball" in cinese, name valid only for specimens without dorsal fin.
- Origin: Cina

- Breeding difficulty: Variable.

◆ ◆ ◆

As the name suggests, this heteromorph is characterized by two "pom poms", i.e. the two soft and round growths that grow near the nostrils.

Each growth (velvet ball, in Chinese) is actually a benign tumor that grows from the epithelial tissue of the animal's nasal septum.

There is a great variety of forms for this breed, ranging from specimens with bodies identical to those of a Fantail to others much more resembling a lion's head or a Ranchu (the true "velvet ball" Pompoms in Chinese aquariology), up to even Celestials equipped with the same

GIUSEPPE BARBONE

# growths.

◆ ◆ ◆

FANCY GOLDFISH

Two Chinese "velvet ball" Pompoms, note the absence of the dorsal fin and the typical final curvature of the spine, also typical of other forms such as the Lion Head (image by Lawrencekhoo).

Given the ubiquity of this characteristic, it would be better to consider it as such, rather than as something that distinguishes a specific breed of goldfish, just as happens with the wen.

In this regard it goes without saying that, as regards the compatibility aspect, it is very variable based on the physical shape of the specimen in front of us.

A Ranchu or a Celestial of the Pompom variety will have the same handicaps (if not greater) as their corresponding starting varieties, swimming and feeding problems far greater than those of a Fantail equipped with the same growths, at least as long as these they will not grow to block their vision or interfere with their feeding.

◆ ◆ ◆

# TELESCOPE

A Black Moor, by far the most widespread and famous telescopic goldfish.

- Names: Telescope goldfish, Demekin, 出目金 (Chū mù jīn) In Chinese.
- Origin: China, around the early 1700s.
- Breeding difficulty: Low.

❖ ❖ ❖

As the name itself suggests, the most striking feature of these fishes is the protruding shape of their eyes.

This form is due to a bilateral benign medulloepithelioma, a rare primary tumor that normally affects the nervous system of many animals, including humans, causing quite a few problems... but which in this variety of goldfish develops only close to the ocular tissue, without causing major side effects in the animal, other than a significant reduction in vision, which varies from specimen to specimen.

The shape of the eyes is itself variable, ranging from fish with conical eyes to others with an almost completely spherical shape.

❖ ❖ ❖

Several variations accepted as standard in competitions (image by N.F. Zolotnitsky (1851 -

FANCY GOLDFISH

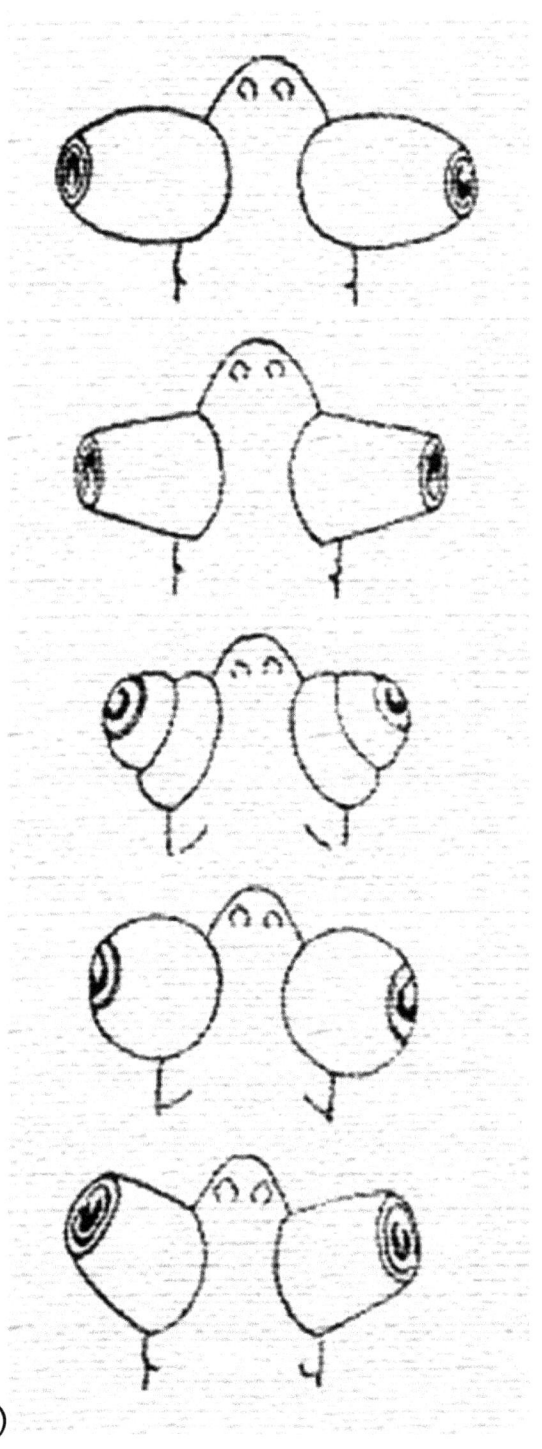

1920)

63

As regards the body of this fish, it can have the typical shape of the Ryukin, with the characteristic humped back, or of the Fantail, the non-melanic varieties (Black Moor) are commonly called Demekin (dragon's eye in Japanese), especially those deriving from the Ryukin.

However, "Demekin" still remains a name commonly used to indicate any type of fish with telescopic eyes or... dragon's eye.

Typical non-melanistic Demekin

(Image By Lawrencekhoo - Own work, CC BY-SA 4.0, https://commons.wikimedia.org/w/index.php?curid=37240409)

The shape of the tails is variable, ranging from specimens with very short tails, similar to a bow, to those with the characteristic veil fins.

Of all the Demekin on the market, Black Moor, or its totally black variety, is the most widespread.

The name, which is entirely a program, refers to the "Moors" of North Africa.

A Black Moor specimen is considered perfect only when it is completely black like velvet, without metallic scales on every part of the body.

Image By Riyad Youssef

Demekin in the "panda" variety, also called "Pandamoor" (imagine By Humanfeather).

As regards the breeding of these fish and, above all, the compatibility with other crucian carp breeds, it will be quite variable based on the characteristics of the individual specimen.

Basically, ALL telescopic heteromorphs have poor vision, due to the bilateral medulloendothelioma that gives them the characteristic protuberant eyes.

The sight can even worsen as the animal grows, until it becomes totally blind.

Finally, other specimens are blind already at birth.

It therefore goes without saying that all telescopic crucians cannot coexist successfully with crucians with well-developed eyesight, because they would have a lower ability to find and eat food, running the risk of decay.

It is therefore very important to put them together with other telescopic or other races, such as celestials and bubble eyes, which also have poor eyesight.

Another consequence that should not be underestimated, of their low (or absent) visual ability, will be the tendency of these fish to potentially bump into every object in the tank.

Woods, rocks and other sharp decorations must be eliminated to avoid abrasions and even worse injuries.

This is something that I recommend doing for all heteromorphic goldfish in general, who with their pleasantly "plump" shape are in fact way clumsier, when swimming, than common heteromorphic goldfish and tend to bump into or even get stuck between furnishings... In fact, not even the plumpest fancy goldfish has the slightest awareness of its own size and roundness... just know this.

# WHAT IS THE "WEN"

The wen is a characteristic growth that tends to cover the head, sometimes partially, only on the upper part, other times totally, of some breeds of heteromorphic goldfish.

As with the pompom and the telescopic eyes, here too we are faced with a benign tumor, specifically of an epithelial nature.

Two Oranda Red Caps, note the showy wen which, as is typical in this variety of Oranda, tends to grow and accumulate especially on the upper part of the head, forming the "red cap". (Image By Lawrencekhoo).

All goldfish equipped with wen require greater care in their breeding than more "basic" forms such as

Fantail, Ryukin or Black Moor.

The wen is prone to infections, the surface of these growths has a convoluted shape (similar to that of the cerebral cortex) and is therefore full of inlets in which dirt and bacteria can nest.

The quality of the water will be a fundamental prerogative; nitrates and nitrites must categorically have a value equal to ZERO.

This rule, which in my opinion should apply to any goldfish and not only, even for the more resistant forms such as the common one, becomes mandatory for the more selected varieties.

The aquarium furnishings must also be adequate: NO FURNISHINGS!

The wen can easily get injured and infected by hitting any

rough or sharp surface.

After all, if you intend to dedicate an aquarium to this type of fish... you should dedicate it to them and that's it.

You don't need furniture to embellish a tank... when there are already fish inside that are living works of art.

Sculptures with fins, shaped by centuries of meticulous selection by the great breeders of the past.

Specimen from Ranchu (Image By Lerdsuwa).

Any decor, as well as harmful, would be wasted with such beautiful fish.

# LIONHEAD

- Name: Lion Head.
- Origin: China, around 1400.
- Breeding difficulty: Medium-high.

One of the rarest to find today, the oldest goldfish breed among those with wen.

The most mythical and MYTHOLOGICAL... of all goldfish!

The lion's head deserves a place of honor in the aquariums, fountains or ponds of any fan of fine goldfish.

Mythological because it was inspired, in its selection, by the appearance of the mythical Chinese Guard Lions, typical figures of Chinese but also Japanese folklore, which have their roots in Indian Buddhism.

(Image Leonard G. at English Wikipedia. - Transferred from en.wikipedia to Commons by IngerAlHaosului using CommonsHelper., CC SA 1.0, https://commons.wikimedia.org/w/index.php?curid=9015454)

Guard lions, often also called "lion-dogs" (especially in Japanese mythology), whose statues (石獅; shíshī, or Stone Lions) decorate many palaces and temples in the Far East.

Guard lions defending the entrance of the Forbidden City (image by Allen Timothy Chang).

(Image by Lawrencekhoo)

The lion's head is in fact characterized, especially in specimens with the best genetics, by a widely developed wen, lumpy and similar to a large raspberry, which should bring to mind the mane of a lion.

A wen whose extension is theoretically greater, in the area of the cheeks and mouth, than that of any Oranda or Ranchu, two other breeds equipped with wen and which derive from the lion's head.

I write "in theory" because, above all thanks to various re-crosses with the Lion's Head, Oranda and Ranchu exist today with equally developed wen and a similar shape, the latter are often also called "Lionchu".

However, the fundamental characteristic that distinguishes, more than any other, a Lion's Head from a Ranchu is the shape of the back and spine.

The Ranchu, although very similar to the Lion's Head, due to the lack of dorsal fin and the well-developed wen, is in fact characterized by a conspicuous hump, as well as a tail that curves downwards.

A Ranchu, note the characteristic shape of the back, curved.

(Image by Lerdsuwa)

◆ ◆ ◆

In the Lionhead, however, the back is nice and straight, with the spine that curves only slightly downwards towards the tail, whose two caudal fins are kept almost straight and never directed downwards.

◆ ◆ ◆

A Lion Head notices how the back is much straighter than the Ranchu.

(Image by Roderick Santos)

◆ ◆ ◆

Regarding the breeding of this breed, it is mandatory to understand that we are dealing with extremely clumsy fish and that they can even develop, over time, vision problems due to an excessive growth of the wen, which can end up covering the eyes... in this regard, there is the practice of "trimming" or "shaving", which consists of cutting the excess wen when it covers the eyes or even the mouth; it therefore goes without saying that fish with such serious limitations can only coexist well with other breeds with similar problems, such as the Ranchu and, naturally, inside a tank devoid of ornaments against which our clumsy... chubby friends can bump and get hurt .

Furthermore, as I have already explained in the chapter dedicated to it, the wen is prone to infections and therefore the quality of the water must always be excellent.

For the rest, healthy specimens of Lion's Head are, all things considered, quite robust and resistant fish.

Many specimens live well outdoors even in the middle of winter, however, as already explained previously, the only way to know if you are dealing with a fish resistant to the cold or not... is to leave it outside without a heater and pray that the "Russian roulette" of winter don't let it dry...

I prefer not to take risks, if you really love your animals do the same too.

❖ ❖ ❖

# RANCHU

Ranchu specimen with blue color. (image by Lawrencekhoo).

- Name: Ranchu ("Dutch Worm" in Japanese).
- Origin: Initially China, later Japan, starting from Lion's Head.
- Breeding difficulty: Medium-high.

❖ ❖ ❖

Arriving in Japan thanks to the Dutch, the first Chinese Ranchu, still very similar to the Lionheads from which they derived, attracted the attention of many Japanese breeders who soon began the selection work that produced the fish we know today.

The back became curved, to the point of resembling a perfect arch, with the caudal peduncle bent downwards and the seven caudal fins also pointing downwards, unlike what is seen in the Lionhead where they remain straight.

The name derives from the uncertain and frenetic way of swimming of these fish which, lacking a dorsal fin, have difficulty staying upright and would tend to "roll", turning over on themselves if it were not for the continuous, frenetic movements of the tail with which they manage to keep themselves upright, frenetic like those of a worm.

As for the term "Dutch", this derives, as already explained before, from the fact that in the historical period in which goldfish arrived in Japan from China, they did so imported by the Dutch; as such, goldfish, like any other good coming from outside, were defined as "Dutch", precisely because these were the only people with whom the Japanese allowed themselves to trade.

The Ranchu very quickly conquered the hearts of the Japanese, to the point that the Ranchu is still defined by them as "The King of Goldfish".

The best examples are still produced

today in the land of the rising sun and... very often they remain there.

The best specimens of Ranchu, as with any other goldfish or Koi carp bred in Japan, rarely leave the country and are more often absorbed by the domestic market.

The dominant aesthetic canon is comparable to that of a Sumo wrestler.

EXTREMELY robust bodies, expressing strength and domination.

Round and harmonious shapes, an expression of balance, poise and elegance.

Of all the heteromorphic breeds that take part in the annual beauty competitions, the Ranchu is by far the one that stands out the most in Japan in terms of number of participants, spectators and prizes up for

◆ ◆ ◆

A magnificent competition specimen. (Image by Lerdsuwa).

The competition standard is

that of a fish that has, as already mentioned, a stocky and massive, but also harmonious, physique.

Perfectly symmetrical, both at the level of the fins and the development of the wen.

Scales as small and regular as possible.

And finally swimming that is not difficult, sinuous and fluid.

Naturally within the limits of what a fish with a body that looks like a potato can do…

The Ranchu, like many other heteromorphs, must be observed from above in order to be better appreciated.

And it is above all through observation from above that the winners are established in competitions.

Perfect example of Ranchu, according to the Japanese standard.

(Image by Miwa Steve)

◆ ◆ ◆

Not only during competitions, but also for the rest of their lives, many Ranchu in Japan are raised in low fountains or ponds, where they are visible only from above, rather than in aquariums or deep ponds, as often happens in the West

(Image by Miwa Steve)

◆ ◆ ◆

Another peculiarity that distinguishes the Ranchu from the Testa Di Leone, from which it derives, lies in the development of the wen which, in the Ranchu, forms characteristic "moustaches" on the sides and above the mouth, while in the Testa Di Leone, as already seen before , grows especially at the height of the cheeks.

As regards the breeding of this fish and its difficulty, it does not differ much from that of the Lionhead; the problems are practically the same... except for a greater risk (only slightly greater) of intestinal constipation, due to the even more stocky and compact shape, a problem that can be prevented with a diet rich in blanched vegetables, at least 3 times a week, which I would like to recommend for any other heteromorph (or even common crucian carp).

❖ ❖ ❖

# ORANDA

Magnificent fully mature specimen of "hooded" Oranda. Note the shape of the abundantly developed wen, especially on the upper part of the head.

(Image By Lawrencekhoo - Own work, CC BY-SA 4.0, https://commons.wikimedia.org/w/index.php?curid=37240412)

- Name: Oranda
- Origin: China-Japan
- Breeding difficulty: Medium to high

◆ ◆ ◆

We finally arrive at Oranda, probably the most famous heteromorph.

the oranda is characterized as already mentioned by the presence of the wen and by a body that can recall that of the Fantail, or even of the Ryukin (deeper and taller, with a humped back) depending on the genetic line from which it derives.

An oranda, specifically a Red Cap, with a RELATIVELY slim body, similar to that of a Fantail. (Image by Noor biology)

Another Oranda equipped, on the contrary, with a much taller and stockier body, like that of Ryukin. (image by Lawrencekhoo).

◆ ◆ ◆

The Oranda were in fact obtained from centuries of selection starting from the fantails, a selection aimed above all at the development of the wen.

The Orandas deriving from the Fantail are characterized by a Wen that develops mostly on the upper part of the head, to form the so-called "hood", which can be of a different color compared to the rest of the body (as in the Oranda red cap, color known as "Tancho") or of the same color.

◆ ◆ ◆

On the top this develops more than in any other heteromorph with wen, giving the animal an appearance similar to a sperm whale.

In some specimens, equipped with particular mutations, this can grow enormously, in a pathological manner, to the point of exceeding the size of the fish itself and causing it to overturn...

In this case "trimming" becomes mandatory, removing the excess wen with scissors, in order to lighten the animal.

The other category of Oranda, which we mentioned before and which is increasingly widespread today, is that of the Oranda with a body much more similar to that of the Ryukin, rather than the Fantail, tall and deep, characterized by a conspicuous hump.

This last type of specimen was obtained mainly by crossing the Ryukin with the Lionhead, other times with the Ranchu and selecting, among the progeny, those that maintained the body of the former, complete with dorsal fin, and the head of the latter .

There are at least two genetic lines of this type, one which takes the name of Oranda Shogun, selected mainly in Thailand, the other is that of the Oranda Yuan-Bao, obtained in China through the same Ryukin+Ranchu cross.

Both are increasingly widespread, thanks to fairly massive exports, to the rest of the world.

The shape of the wen in these fish is totally different from that of the classic oranda seen previously, much more similar to that of the Ranchu or the Lion's Head from which it derives, with a much more uniform growth over the entire face and head. of the animal.

♦ ♦ ♦

Magnificent specimen of Thai Oranda, also called Oranda Shogun.

(Image by Lawrencekhoo).

◆ ◆ ◆

Over the centuries there are many chromatic and morphological varieties, which have been created by human selection, concerning the Oranda; Below you will find the most common ones

Oranda azuma nishiki, characterized by a livery similar to calico, but tending towards blue/violet and with pearly scales.

Oranda red-cap, one of the most famous and easily available; characterized by a pearly white body and a red wen that grows on the top of the head.

Oranda with telescopic eyes; obtained from the crossing of Oranda with Demekin.

Oranda hana fusa, or Pompom oranda, a Pompom with a dorsal fin and a wen at the same time, is obtained by crossing a classic Oranda with a Pompom with a Fantail body.

The Nagate Oranda, a Japanese

variety from the province of Shikoku, characterized by a long body rather than stocky and round, as is usually typical of heteromorphs.

Oranda Apache, characterized by a black and red livery.

Oranda Panda, white in color with black spots reminiscent of those of pandas.

Oranda Chakin (チャキ, or red tea fish, in Japanese), also called chocolate oranda, characterized by chocolate-colored scales, its Japanese name always refers to the color, which can recall that of black tea.

Oranda Seibungyo (成分魚) or Seibun, or Blue Oranda.

Black Oranda, obtained from

a cross with Black Moor.

Jade seal oranda, almost a Red Cap "in reverse", with a white cap and an orange body.

◆ ◆ ◆

As far as the breeding of these fish is concerned, the Oranda is positioned more or less in the same category as the Lionhead and the Ranchu.

Although less limited in movement, they are still often subject to problems with the functioning of the swim bladder, due to the often extremely short body shape and, consequently, due to the excessive compression of the internal organs.

A diet rich in fiber and low in cereals, which I recommend for every crucian carp, becomes more than obligatory for these fish; very often mistreated in terms of nutrition (and not only) simply because they are more widespread and common than other elaborate varieties, such as the aforementioned Ranchu and Lionhead, as well as sold, at least for the low quality and more "commercial" specimens, to lower prices.

In addition to nutrition, the sore point of Oranda is also the quality of the water; nitrites and nitrates must be ZERO, I will never tire of repeating this...

This applies to every goldfish and even more so to those with wen, which are very prone to infections.

The tub must be as free of furniture as possible.

REAL plants are fine, as long as

you are able to find ones resistant to the FURIOUS AND COMPULSIVE hunger of these fishes… (I have seen heteromorphs tear apart and devour Anubias and even Echinodorus, so… Good luck!).

◆ ◆ ◆

Just like all other highly selected goldfish, I also advise against breeding Orandas outdoors in winter, unless you have a heater that keeps the water around 15 degrees.

Finally, as regards compatibility, Orandas should be placed together with other goldfish whose swimming is similarly impaired, which I recommend judging from fish to fish, as there is in fact a great physical variability, as we have seen, in this breed.

◆ ◆ ◆

# PEARLSCALE

- Name: Pearl scales, Golf ball fish.
- Origin: China
- Breeding difficulty: High.

Image By Lawrencekhoo - Own work, CC BY-SA 4.0, https://commons.wikimedia.org/w/index.php?curid=37240414

◆ ◆ ◆

Among all the heteromorphs, which, as we have seen, are already characterized by a fairly stocky and round physique, the Pearl Scales definitely stands out above all, with a body that, in some specimens, becomes , wider than long.

In addition to the special silhouette, which would be enough to make it unique, this cute fat guy is characterized by curious calcified thickenings, close to each scale, which make the scales similar to pearls and which give the entire animal a similar appearance. to that of a golf ball.

## Pearlscale with wen

(Image By Lerdsuwa - Own photo (400D + 50/1.4), CC BY-SA 3.0, https://commons.wikimedia.org/w/index.php?curid=1781691)

Pearlscale are particularly prone to problems resulting from swim bladder compression, given their extremely round body shape.

(Image By Michelle Jo - Own work, CC BY-SA 3.0, https://commons.wikimedia.org/w/index.php?curid=15610144)

◆ ◆ ◆

Four servings of blanched vegetables a week are mandatory.

Given the great inability in swimming, it should be held to other

heteromorphs equally penalized by own morphology, such as Ranchu, Bubble Eyes and Celestials.

Like any other race seen so far, nothing prevents a pearlscale from also having telescopic eyes and/or wen, thus adding other visual/physical disabilities as well as greater sensitivity to the quality of the water.

The quality of the water is perhaps more important for this breed than for any other, not only must nitrates and nitrites be zero, but the acidity of the water must be quite low, with a pH as neutral as possible; this applies to every goldfish, even more so to the Pearlscale, in order to avoid corrosion of the calcium thickenings, which cover the scales.

◆ ◆ ◆

# BUBBLE EYE

Specimen of "Bubble eye", note the characteristic under-ocular bags.

(Image By Angie Torres from Toronto - extra flotation devices, CC BY-SA 2.0, https://commons.wikimedia.org/w/index.php?curid=10724404)

-Name: Bubble Eyes

-Origin: China

- Breeding difficulty: High

◆ ◆ ◆

We now land in the realm of the grotesque, with the bubble-eyed goldfish.

The world of "Fancy Goldfish" owners is divided between those who love them and those who hate them or, better said, hate the kind of selection that led to the birth of this breed.

Bubble eyes are characterized by two large sacs filled with fluid immediately under the eyes.

The sacs, which appear in the first months of the fish's development, continue to grow, reaching their final size (sometimes even very large) with the complete maturation of the animal.

These sacs can have variable dimensions based on the genetic strain, with some specimens developing and maintaining relatively small sacs throughout their lives, and others in which they grow a lot, as in the specimen you see in the photo at the beginning of this chapter.

Bubble Eyes derives from varieties also equipped with sub-ocular sacs, but smaller in size, such as the so-called "Toad Head" goldfish, very similar to our fish but with smaller sacs.

FANCY GOLDFISH

"Toadhead" goldfish, the ancestor from which bubble eyes derives (image by lienyuan lee).

◆ ◆ ◆

The swimming of the animal is considerably impeded, naturally, by similar structures and so is the view, with the eyes perpetually projected upwards, suspended by the large sacs full of fluid below.

Image by Lerdsuwa

◆ ◆ ◆

These sacs are also particularly delicate and vulnerable to impacts, they can in fact easily be punctured by hitting sharp or jagged objects and, although they heal without problems, the wounds are prone to infection.

Studies are currently underway in Japan on the regenerating properties of the fluid contained in the sacs of this fish; in fact, it is thought that it may contain some promoter of cellular growth, which accelerates the healing process of the sacs themselves, every time they are perforated, due to impact against something.

Such research could lead to a

breakthrough in the field of human tissue regeneration and the treatment of regenerative diseases, as well as of course in the rehabilitation of people seriously injured following accidents.

If you decide to buy these fish, the good old rule of not putting furniture in the tank becomes absolutely mandatory with this breed, given that the slightest sharp object, such as wood, rocks, amphorae, etc... can tear the delicate sub-ocular sacs.

At most you can place a few well-polished river stones at the bottom of the pool, but nothing more.

◆ ◆ ◆

Other physical characteristics of this breed are the lack of dorsal fin (but not always) and the "three-tailed" shape of the caudal fin; that is, a double caudal fin, as in almost all heteromorphs, but which keeps the two upper lobes of the two tails joined together, giving the entire tail the appearance of a three-bladed helix.

Other "particular signs" are the tendency of this breed to not grow as much as the others and to remain relatively small, with maximum lengths of around 15cm.

◆ ◆ ◆

As regards the compatibility of this fish with other breeds, it should be placed exclusively with other bubble eyes or at most with other visually impaired breeds, such as the Demekin and the Celestials (which we will talk about in the next chapter).

I recommend placing them exclusively with the latter, as well as with their peers, given that in addition to being visually impaired they are also significantly impaired in swimming, decidedly more so than demekins.

As for outdoor living, even in this case we recommend using a heater in winter.

◆ ◆ ◆

# CELESTIAL

(image by JasonMarini)

- Names: Celestials, Choutengan, Celestial Eyes
- Origins: Uncertain between China or Korea, starting with 18th century telescopes.
- Breeding difficulty: High.

◆ ◆ ◆

Celestials are a breed of goldfish characterized by the bizarre shape of their eyes, perpetually "staring at the sky", due to a mutation that led some Demekin to have their telescopic eyes pointing upwards, rather than to the sides as normally happens.

FANCY GOLDFISH

Group of Celestials (Photo by Michelle Jo)

❖ ❖ ❖

Basically they are therefore telescopic, i.e. goldfish affected by bilateral medulloepithelioma, but with their eyes turned upwards.

More specifically, according to one theory, the Celestial could also derive from the "Toad Head" (Hama-tou in Japanese), just like the Bubble Eyes, given the orientation of the eyes (upwards) and the body shape similar to both Toadhead and Bubble Eyes; in this case therefore, the Celestial would have evolved from Toadhead affected by Medulloepithelioma, like the Demekin, or from crosses between the Toadhead and the latter.

Other typical characteristics are the lack of dorsal and the tail pointing slightly downwards, with the double caudal fin that opens horizontally.

The dimensions, as for the Bubble Eyes

and the Toad Head, are not very large, the body remains particularly slender, making the Celestial a superior and more lively swimmer than other dorsal varieties, such as the Lion Head and Ranchu.

As far as compatibility is concerned, this breed should also be placed possibly only with its peers; if you want to get too far... you could at most put it together with Bubble Eyes and a few Demekins.

Among the Heteromorph breeds, it is one of the most susceptible to low temperatures, therefore it should be kept outdoors only with a heater.

❖ ❖ ❖

# REPRODUCTION

The reproduction of fancies, and goldfish more generally, is not something as difficult as many beginners tend to think; to tell the truth, in a tank, or better yet in a pond, large enough and populated, it becomes quite easy to find new specimens from time to time.

Crucian carp are externally reproducing fish, this means that they reproduce in the following way: Females lay eggs and males fertilize them with their sperm.

The mating season for goldfish is typically in spring however, as with many other domesticated animals, it is enough to have multiple breedings during the year.

In goldfish, males are distinguished from females by having a head that is proportionally larger than the body, as well as squarer than that of the female, and a generally thinner body.

Females, on the contrary, have smaller, thinner heads and a plumper body, with a more rounded belly.

In heteromorphs, however, the distinction made on the basis of body proportions becomes more difficult given that, due to human selection, the development of a stocky and voluminous body has been favored in females as much as in males.

However, there is a bodily characteristic, typical of males and absent in females, in homomorphs as well as in heteromorphs, namely the so-called "nuptial tubercles".

As the name suggests, they are precisely tubercles, greyish-white in colour, which appear during the fregola, specifically covering the gill covers and the head of the males, sometimes also extending to the rest of the body, albeit in smaller quantities.

In fully mature males, once a certain age has passed, the tubercles tend to remain even in the non-reproductive period, effectively becoming permanent.

◆ ◆ ◆

**Detail of the tubercles in a male goldfish** (image by Pogrebnoj-Alexandroff).

◆ ◆ ◆

Even more than the appearance, an unmistakable clue, which will be of great help to you in understanding the sex of your fish, is the typical behavior that males display as soon as they perceive the presence of a female full of eggs.

In fact, the males will chase your females throughout the tank, trying to "crush" them against the walls and furnishings, pressing with their heads on the female's body, in an attempt to push the female to lay.

If the male is larger than the female, or there are more males chasing one, the latter may be in serious danger; it is not uncommon for a group of males or a particularly vigorous one to harm the female, pressing her and bumping her against the tank furnishings or even against the filter.

All the more reason not to put any kind of sharp or hard furnishings in your oranda aquarium.

My advice is, once you have identified the breeding pair, put the two fish in a separate tank, even a small one as long as it is equipped with an oxygenator, completely empty except for something soft but quite rough, on which to let the female lay her eggs .

Fish eggs are in fact sticky and adhere to surfaces

Goldfish eggs (image by Michelle Jo)

◆ ◆ ◆

Goldfish EAT their own eggs, and their own children.

Which is why, if you want to reproduce them in adequate numbers, it is a good idea to put the breeding pair in a separate tank; the point is to keep them in a controlled environment, so as to be able to better monitor the stages of reproduction and remove the fish once they have spawned.

Once the eggs have been laid and covered with sperm by the male, the water in the breeding tank will be cloudy and milky due to the seminal fluid dissolved in it.

Wait a couple of hours to make sure that fertilization has taken place, then proceed to change the water, replacing it with water from the aquarium of our breeders (the same water with which you filled the tank from the beginning), making sure that the temperature is the same, to avoid temperature changes.

◆ ◆ ◆

Change the water periodically, always with water from your aquarium, and never remove the oxygenator.

Water changes are essential since, in a breeding tank, you can't use the filter... unless you want to suck up eggs and fry.

Continue like this and, if the eggs are fertile and not moldy, after a few days they will hatch, giving life to your fry.

Goldfish fry (image by Michelle Jo)

◆ ◆ ◆

The larvae (this is the name given to the fry of externally fertilized fish, as well as amphibians) will have a very different appearance from the adults, as you can clearly see in the previous images, and their food needs will also be different.

In the first 1-2 days they will not feed, as they are still nourished by the yolk sac of their egg, which remains attached to the belly, from which it will be reabsorbed.

Once this phase is over, they will need to feed, I recommend giving them baby brine shrimp, i.e. the very small newborns of brine shrimp (the famous "sea monkeys") whose eggs are now available in every aquarium shop as fish food, often in packages equipped with hatching sets.

I therefore recommend taking

precautions beforehand, rather than struggling after our fry have already been born, with the risk of making them starve to death.

Alternatively, there are now also feeds for fry, in the form of pulverized dry food; However, I recommend artemia nauplii as the food of choice, given the great attraction they have on fry of any species.

This is what your fry will look like after two months (image by Michelle Jo)

◆ ◆ ◆

In any case, after 2-3 weeks, you can already feed your little fish with the same food you use for the parents, but being careful to chop it up to make it within reach of their little mouths.

In the meantime, it is very important to continue changing the water every day, checking the water values, especially nitrates and nitrites, several times a day and always keeping the oxygenator running.

Your fish will be too small to fit in a tank with a filter for at least two months...

Taking care of the reproduction of goldfish requires a lot of effort and dedication, in any case a large number of eggs and fish will die, no matter how assiduous your care may be... considering however the high numbers involved (a female also lays thousands of eggs... ) if you take enough care, barring unforeseen circumstances, you will still end up with a few dozen fish.

A method to have even more control over reproduction is that of the so-called "squeezing"; that is, literally squeezing the eggs out of your female, into the breeding tank, then squeezing the male into it and then mixing well in order to encourage the union of the sperm with the eggs.

Some breeders prefer to squeeze the male twice, both before squeezing the female, thus dyeing the water with the seminal fluid beforehand, and later, after squeezing the female.

❖ ❖ ❖

Squeezing is a technique that requires EXTREME delicacy on the part of those who perform it, however it is not excessively difficult; it essentially involves holding the fish still with one hand, placing it belly up to the air, so as to expose the belly, and massaging the belly with a finger, pressing and pushing slightly towards the anus, so as to push the eggs or the seminal fluid out of the oviduct or sperm duct, both positioned just before the anal opening.

The advantage of squeezing is that you naturally have complete control over the laying of eggs and their fertilization, all without the risk of the parents themselves eating the eggs... as easily happens when they are left to do it themselves.

Furthermore, in some cases, when the females full of eggs for any reason are unable to lay, it becomes an obligatory action if one wants to avoid complications for the female, due to the retention of the eggs which, if they are not completely reabsorbed (something that can quite frequently happen) would begin to rot inside the female's body, causing infection.

◆ ◆ ◆

A trick to stimulate fregola in goldfish is to simulate the arrival of spring.

As mentioned previously, the arrival of spring represents a great stimulus to the reproduction of crucian carp.

A good method to simulate it is to keep our fish with little food for a couple of weeks (nothing drastic, feeding them once a day instead of two-three will have the effect) and then continue feeding them more abundantly, especially with bloodworms and fresh food in general, both animal and vegetable, and progressively increase the temperature of the aquarium by one degree every week.

An increase of even just two degrees, combined with an increase in the quantity and variety of food, will be enough to convince your fish that we are moving from winter to spring; this will lead to females producing eggs and males producing sperm.

This method is particularly successful in winter, given that we start from temperatures that are already objectively low.

❖ ❖ ❖

# CONCLUSIONS

I want to dedicate this last chapter of my book to ethical considerations.

Anyone who buys a goldfish must understand that what they have in their hands is an animal, an animal not only capable of feeling pain but also endowed with a certain intelligence which, as such, must be stimulated.

Prisons like the damned ampoules... or even mini-aquariums, are real torture chambers for fish that need to swim and that grow, as I already wrote at the beginning of this book, a LOT too.

A common goldfish needs at least one hundred liters to feel good, taking into account its growth, sixty in the case of the stockier and clumsier heteromorphs, such as Oranda and similar.

As already said, a goldfish lives better (and much better) if it is in company.

Goldfish are social animals, they live in schools where they recognize each other and also develop a feeding hierarchy (this is what you are seeing when you observe two goldfish chasing each other and head bumping each other, after you give them food), after a few days of having purchased them they will recognize your voice, as well as your face, among those of anyone else.

They will run to you for food and will flee if they see or hear unfamiliar faces and voices.

Heteromorphs then, I write from personal experience, will even let you touch them and will do so of their own free will, if you are kind and never abrupt with them.

I was lucky enough to own an Oranda in the past who was practically a little dog with fins...

A happy goldfish, because it lives in a large enough tank and is stimulated by company, will be physically MUCH healthier, will develop very few infections throughout its life and will live much longer.

What I want you to understand is that my considerations on the "psychological" well-being of these animals are not something thrown out there, by an unhinged animal rights fanatic, or even worse an easy bait for tender-hearted people, launched only to sell more copies (I don't think I would put this in the book's end otherwise... given that, if you are reading me now, you have already bought the book), but rather objective advice that will allow you to live your experience in a more relaxed and better way, precisely because you won't have to deal with fishes that will get sick every day.

In fish, perhaps more than in any other animal, stress and the cortisol produced in response to it drastically lower the immune defenses, making them more vulnerable to all kinds of infections.

Having said that, once this exquisitely "mechanistic" parenthesis has been extinguished, I still remain of the opinion that an animal HAS THE RIGHT TO BE HAPPY, to live the best possible life that we can offer it, and I would think so even if we lived in an ideal world, where unhappiness and stress have no effect on a fish's immune defenses.

Another consideration, of an ethical nature, that I want to make is one relating to the different breeds of heteromorphs examined so far and the kind of selection that man has carried out on these, to the point of producing varieties with an aberrant appearance (to be kind).

I won't be melodramatic about it, I simply believe that the selection of characters that increase the probability of injury and related infection, such as bubble eyes just to name one... or the selection of excessively bulky and compact bodies, like that of the Pearl scale , which significantly increases the risk of constipation and subsequent swim bladder malfunction, are not something I find one hundred percent ethical (understatement).

In any case, I will not tear my clothes in front of anyone who decides to buy and breed these fish, basically any breed of heteromorph, even the Bubble Eye, or the Celestial, with its visually impaired eyes constantly turned upwards. ... can still have a healthy and dignified life, as long as those who own them respect EVERY SINGLE NEED that these breeds of fish, particularly handicapped by human selection, require.

I have seen in my life many more Bubble Eyes, Celestials, etc. lead frighteningly better lives than those of many common goldfish, much more agile and capable, not at all handicapped by human selection, but condemned, thanks to the very low price range and to the reputation of being "easy fish" that they carry around, leading a BRIEF and

MISERABLE existence, in the most unspeakable tanks and in the hands of the most incompetent "aquarists".

And all this, paradoxically, thanks to that same human selection, which has made many heteromorphs mediocre swimmers… but at the same time also rare valuable breeds.

As the good old Morpheus would say: "As we know… Fate, it seems, is not without a sense of irony…"

And to anyone who wants to insist on the fact that certain

varieties of goldfish would never survive in nature anyway...

I want to remind them that goldfish are DOMESTIC ANIMALS, as such they are not expected to survive in nature, because they are animals that They MUST NOT live in the wild; as an invasive and non-native species, in practically every natural habitat in the world.

In conclusion therefore, my advice is to ONLY buy the breeds that you know you can handle.

In fact, I can even go so far as to say that the real difference between an "easy" breed (so to speak... as we have abundantly seen) and one that is difficult to manage is made by the person who takes care of these fish.

If you are an attentive aquarist, with some knowledge of the variety you choose, armed with the right patience and dedication to keep up with his needs, you will be able to give him a happy and peaceful existence.

For example, the same cannot be said for some dog breeds that have been particularly "botched" by human selection, such as bulldogs, pugs or dachshunds.

No heteromorphic goldfish, however heavily handicapped by human selection, will have difficulty breathing... or suffer from a myriad of potential heart diseases... or, again, have a marked predisposition to diabetes...

The same cannot be said for any of the dog breeds mentioned above.